3/4/96   */1/96   15†

Four Corners Country

Smoked Ceiling, Spruce Tree House, Mesa Verde, Colorado

Four Corners Country

Photographs by Dick Arentz

Text by Ian Thompson

Foreword by Philip Hyde

The University of Arizona Press / Tucson

About the Photographer

Dick Arentz began serious use of the large format camera in 1969 and since that time his work has been exhibited in nearly thirty one-man shows in the United States and Europe and is in permanent collections on both continents. His portfolios have included studies of Death Valley and Zion National Park. He has taught photography at Northern Arizona University in Flagstaff, Arizona.

About the Author

Ian Thompson grew up in the Four Corners Country of Colorado and New Mexico. He has written extensively on the natural and cultural history of the region. He has been editor of *The Durango Herald* and *The Silverton Standard and The Miner*, both in southwest Colorado, and has served as mayor of the town of Durango. He is executive director of the Crow Canyon Archaeological Center in Cortez, Colorado.

To Ewald Arentz and Amy Thompson

THE UNIVERSITY OF ARIZONA PRESS

Copyright © 1986, The Arizona Board of Regents, All Rights Reserved. Manufactured in the U.S.A.
Photographs copyright © 1986 by Dick Arentz

Library of Congress Cataloging-in-Publication Data: Thompson, Ian (Ian M.) Four Corners Country
1. Four Corners Region—Description and travel—Views.   I. Arentz, Dick.   II. Title.
F788.5.T47   1986   978   86-11397 ISBN 0-8165-0920-4 (alk. paper)

Contents

Foreword

Traditional photography has been considered by most people to have two primary characteristics: optical clarity of the image produced and smooth rendition of tone and texture—in short, a "good" photograph rendered an image that closely resembled what the perceptive human eye might see. This school of realism is alive and well and is even thriving in many parts of the country, most notably in the western United States, where nature perhaps more profoundly influences people's lives.

Dick Arentz's photographs are striking in their seeing and mastery of photographic technique. The seeing is strongly individual and is suffused with confidence. Though Dick is of a later generation than the "old masters," his work is in the classic tradition of photographic realism. His photographs do honor to the prime characteristics of the medium. They serve as a reminder of the beauty of black-and-white and its special attractions.

Ian Thompson's text complements the photographs well, setting them in the context of the country portrayed, and synthesizing the region's history—the long geological perspective, followed by the story of the succession of people who came into the country.

The beauty and subtlety of *Four Corners Country* will be appreciated by those who will take the time to let their eyes journey slowly through these pages.

PHILIP HYDE

7

Four Corners Country

Four Corners Country

From the peaks of the San Juan Mountains the country plunges thousands of feet, levels briefly to sweep across the mesas, then breaks and plunges again into the far, shimmering basins. Rock as far as the eye can see.

The Four Corners Country we call it, this place where Arizona, Colorado, New Mexico, and Utah meet. It has had other names before, uttered in forgotten tongues. It is a place of rearing, plunging, freezing, scorching rock, not an easy place for life to find a roothold or a toehold. Yet life, in a multitude of forms, does cling to this vast sweep of stone.

The center of the Four Corners Country is marked by a monument where the corners of the four states come together on a sere and rubbled plain just south of the San Juan River. The outer boundaries of the Four Corners Country are more difficult to define. Those boundaries surround the people who consider themselves residents of the region.

The heartland of the Four Corners Country is the San Juan River Basin, a twenty-five-thousand-square-mile expanse of peaks and brilliant mesas and canyons draining into the San Juan River which joins the Colorado River at the foot of Navajo Mountain in Utah. Surrounding the San Juan basin are other river drainages whose inhabitants speak of themselves as living in the Four Corners Country. They include the valleys of the Dolores and upper Gunnison rivers in the north, the upper Rio Grande in the east, a segment of the Colorado River in the west, and the Little Colorado River in the south.

Though the region is vast, not many people call it home. The Four Corners Country remains one of the most sparsely populated, rugged, and remote parts of the United States. The lack of population is balanced, however, by an intricate historical and cultural mosaic shaped by the land.

The first people came into the region less than ten thousand years ago, later than was true of most of the continent. They were mobile, small bands of hunters and gatherers following far-flung, cyclical routes between the mountains, mesas, and canyons.

Two thousand years ago, after the dawn of agriculture here, the Four Corners was the birthplace of the Anasazi civilization, whose people called this place home for over a thousand years before they departed. They left behind the stone towns preserved today in Mesa Verde and Chaco national parks and Aztec, Canyon de Chelly, Navajo, and Hovenweep national monuments. The Anasazi joined other ancestral peoples along the Rio Grande or on the Hopi Mesas where their descendants live today.

Following the departure of the Anasazi from their ancient San Juan homeland, the nomadic Navajos and Jicarilla Apaches entered the region south of the San Juan River, and the fleet-footed Utes came into the northern region of the Four Corners Country. All these tribes remain here today.

By the mid-sixteenth century the Four Corners Country lay within Spain's New World empire. In the early nineteenth century possession of the Four Corners Country passed from Spain to Mexico and, in 1848, it was part of the territory ceded to the United States by Mexico.

The Rivers

To the modern mind struggling to impose logic upon nature, finding the connection between the towering peaks and the sandy lowlands, between the chill and treeless tundra swathing the highest ridges and the sparse grasslands of the lowland basins, might seem hopeless. But, pulsing like open arteries cut deep into the weathered sinew of the rock, the rivers reveal themselves.

Rather than the Four Corners Country, this region might better be called the Five Rivers Country. It is the rivers which shape the stone and the lives of this place. Four of those rivers—the Rio Grande, the San Juan, the Dolores, and the Gunnison—begin among the fourteen-thousand-foot peaks of the San Juan Mountains in southwestern Colorado. The fifth river, the Colorado, arcs down from the north to form the western perimeter of the Four Corners Country.

Of the five rivers, only the Rio Grande flows eastward toward the Gulf of Mexico and the Atlantic. The San Juan, Dolores, and Gunnison all join the Colorado in its thundering southwestward rush toward the Pacific.

Before the rivers, however, came the basic stuff of the Four Corners Country, the rock. The oldest rock, ancient beyond imagining, is metamorphic. Its role in shaping today's Four Corners Country is as great as its age. Yet this oldest rock remains the most elusive, least evident of all stone in the region. In the Four Corners Country it reveals itself only in the higher reaches of a great dome, the San Juan uplift, which has been ravaged and battered by the seasons to form the rugged San Juan Mountains.

The San Juan Range and other major uplifts in the region have not been a permanent part of the Four Corners Country. The forces which slowly heaved up the earth's crust from which today's Four Corners Country is carved had been at work before. Each time the uplifts occurred, erosion relentlessly tore the domes away and scattered the debris across the basins to lay down yet another layer of sedimentary rock in endless repetition. The uplifts are being worn down once more, at this moment.

The slowness of the recurring uplifts has been matched by another slow-paced drama which for two billion years has contributed mightily to the rocky character of the country—that is the inching advance and retreat of a succession of oceans over this place. The oceans have come in from the west and returned to the west at a rate of only a few feet every million years. Each ocean had plenty of time to lay down new sediments that were pressed into rock layers hundreds of feet thick.

The age of the oldest rock is difficult to determine; some may predate life itself. The oldest exposed rock, that found along and above the Animas Canyon north of Durango, may be more than two billion years old. Because it lacks evidence of life and has been so transformed by heat and pressure, this rock reveals little about its age and origin.

It is possible that it was laid down by an ocean following what was to

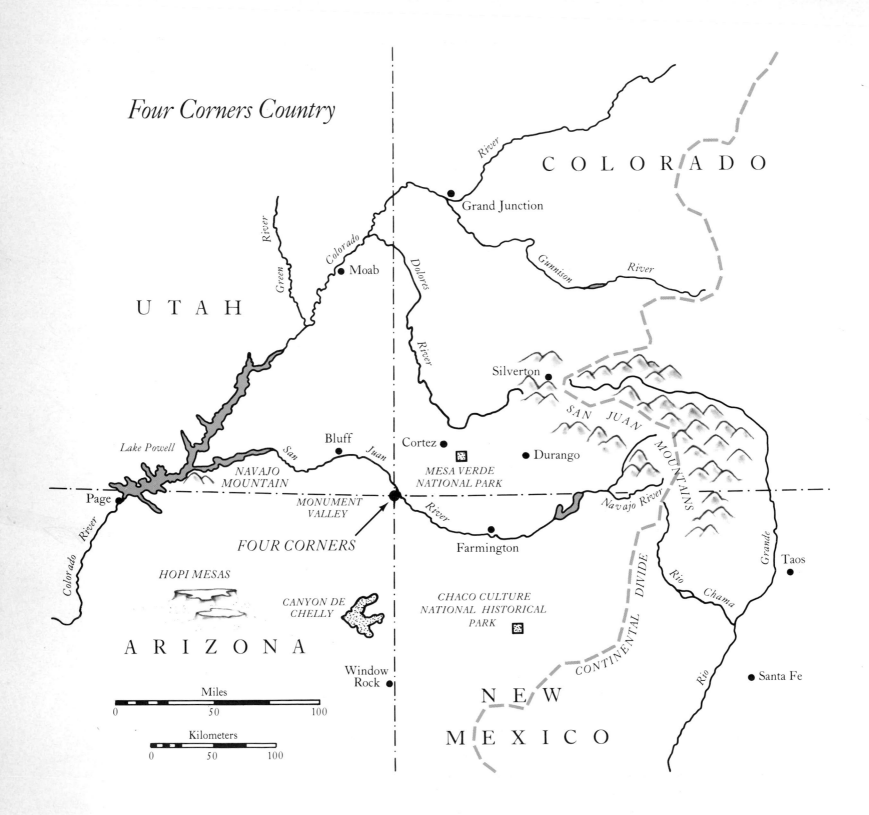

Four Corners Country

COLORADO

River

Grand Junction

UTAH

Green River

Colorado River

Moab

Dolores River

Gunnison River

Lake Powell

San

Bluff

Juan

Cortez

Durango

Silverton

SAN JUAN MOUNTAINS

NAVAJO MOUNTAIN

Page

MONUMENT VALLEY

FOUR CORNERS

MESA VERDE NATIONAL PARK

River

Navajo River

Colorado River

HOPI MESAS

CANYON DE CHELLY

CHACO CULTURE NATIONAL HISTORICAL PARK

Farmington

CONTINENTAL DIVIDE

Rio Chama

Rio Grande

Taos

ARIZONA

Window Rock

NEW

Santa Fe

MEXICO

Rio

Miles

0   50   100

Kilometers

0   50   100

become the usual route for the advance and retreat of seas across this region, up from the west and back again toward the coast of what is now California.

In the intervals between the presence of oceans, wind-borne sand, piled into dunes hundreds of feet thick, formed new rock, or slow meandering rivers deposited sediments upon the land between the dome and the beaches of advancing or retreating seas.

Six hundred million years ago the seas brought something new: teeming life that was to leave behind stone of its own. The massive layers of chalky limestones are the compressed remains of limy shells and skeletons of trillions of sea creatures settling to and dying upon the floors of forgotten seas.

Two hundred fifty million years ago, during the Permian, a great sea lapped at the Four Corners Country lowlands. Its beach was deep, white sand now cemented as the creamy Cedar Mesa Sandstone from which so much of Canyonlands National Park is sculpted.

As the Permian sea began its retreat, rivers from the nearby highlands meandered across muggy tidal flats, laying down the soft, brilliant Chinle and Moenkopi sediments found atop the Permian landscape where they have not been swept from the harder rock by erosion. Those Triassic-age rivers carried logs down from inland forests and left them in great logjams at every meander so that today the Moenkopi and Chinle formations are studded with chunks of petrified wood. Later, some of those logs soaked up uranium-saturated fluids, a phenomenon that was to have a profound impact upon some cultures of the Four Corners millions of years later.

The uplifts rose higher above the Moenkopi and Chinle mudflats and the rivers flowed faster across the flats. For tens of millions of years, ending about 175 million years ago, Triassic rivers and winds swept iron-rich debris from the uplifts and laid it down upon the Chinle to create the deep, rusty layer of Wingate Sandstone which forms the inner gorge of the middle Dolores Canyon, hems in much of Lake Powell, towers above Canyonlands, and dominates other remote expanses of the Four Corners Country.

Later, the wind-borne Entrada and Navajo sandstones of the Jurassic Period of 150 million years ago were deposited. The Entrada is the

15

across the foothills; junipers, piñon pine, and sagebrush took root in the deep mesa soils; grasses held the basin soils against the spring winds, and box elder, hackberry, reeds, willows, and cacti grew along the canyon bottoms.

And a thousand more kinds of grass, shrub, tree, bird, mammal, and reptile took on forms suited to this stone, these seasons, and to one another.

Because the Four Corners Country drops from peaks that jut more than fourteen thousand feet into the frosty sky down to arid elevations below four thousand feet in the canyon bottoms, this region nurtures life zones ranging from those of the Alaskan interior to the Mexican interior.

Temperature and elevation are not the only contributors to this ecological diversity. Annual snow and rainfall ranges from great abundance in the mountains to scarcity in the desert basins.

One can sit on a tundra-covered peak and look down on the alpine forests and across the sage-blanketed mesas to where the land breaks into shimmering basins. On a long summer's day one can walk through all the ecosystems of the Four Corners Country.

Mountains, Mesas, Canyons

Within the cosmos of the Four Corners Country there are three levels: Mountain, Mesa, and Canyon. The rivers and rock lead from one plane to the next. When viewed from the hot basins, the mountains appear as welcome mirages, upper worlds capped by snow, cooled by shadowy forests. They rise, a chill and distant blue, above the red rocks of the canyon rims, their peaks floating above the vast pastel sweeps of the plateaus.

One's eyes are raised to them and one's path may quite unconsciously turn toward them. The mountains exert a gravity of their own upon the human psyche. The peaks are the source of the cool rivers flowing between the mesas. The towering ridges attract the cooling dusk breezes that soothe the heat-stricken land.

In the north the massive San Juan Mountains dominate the land. In them begin the rivers and their tributaries—the Piedra, Pine, Florida, Animas, La Plata, and Mancos—all flowing into the San Juan; the

Uncompahgre flowing into the Gunnison; the San Miguel flowing into the Dolores, and the Chama flowing southeastward into the Rio Grande. In the east the Sangre de Cristos, beyond the Rio Grande, define the far boundaries of the Four Corners Country, shadowing at dawn the Pueblo villages along the great river and the ancient Hispanic towns clinging to the hills above the Rio Grande and the Chama. In the west the La Sals, the Abajos, and Navajo Mountain rise from the rims of the Colorado River canyons, forming the backdrop for the chasms carved into the brilliant sandstones of Utah and Arizona. In the south the basins are flanked by the Zuni Mountains and Black Mesa and are bisected by the Carrizos, the Lukachukais, and the Chuskas. The Sleeping Ute and the La Platas rise from within the basins.

Except from the bottoms of the canyons, there is nowhere in the Four Corners Country from which at least one of the ranges is not visible, its presence not felt. But that is to see them from a distance. From afar they are weightless, floating on the sweep of the mesas, the resting place of the circle of sky upon the circle of earth.

The middle level of the Four Corners Country, where the stone levels before breaking into the basins, is ruled by the mesas. Poised between mountain and canyon country, the mesas are more than mere planes of transition. They possess a gentle character of their own. They are the temperate zone.

The mesas, and broad river valleys separating them, are the places where, since the dawn of agriculture here more than two thousand years ago, people have gathered to push back the wildness for fields, homes, and towns.

The natural gentleness of many mesas has been made more inviting by the farms and orchards that spread across them and over the low ridges and quiet hollows. Where ditches bring water up from the rivers, the rolling fields are in pasture or planted with corn and alfalfa. Curving ranks of cottonwoods grow along the ditches and in the rocky, shallow bottoms to shade the houses and barns of families now as deeply rooted in the mesa soils as the trees themselves. Beyond the ditches, after the water has run out, vast checkerboards of golden winter wheat, red fallow fields, and green pinto beans cover the mesas from the foothills of the mountains to the canyon rims.

But not all the mesas have submitted to plow and axe. Some remain, rising above the canyons, as wild as were all the mesas before the first kernels of maize were pushed deep into their soils millennia ago.

Cutting between the mesas and deep into the basin floors are the canyons of Four Corners Country. To the wanderer they are much like cathedrals, not raised above the earth to dominate the surrounding fields and forests, but sunk into the very stone that forms their walls.

Some of the canyons, like de Chelly and Tsegi in Arizona or the Rio Grande Gorge in New Mexico or the Dolores in Colorado, are cut deep into mesas and plateaus. Others, like the Goosenecks of the San Juan in Utah, are deep and resounding chasms gouged deep into basin floors.

These canyons are worlds of their own. The climate in the bottom is markedly different from that on the rim. Water may be nonexistent above and plentiful in the shadowy warmth below. The result can be an oasis stretching along the canyon floor that would be hard for the traveler of the country beyond the rims to imagine.

With their great length and sheer walls, the canyons are the greatest barriers to straight-line travel across much of the Four Corners. On the other hand they are passages for rivers and life between the peaks and basins. The canyons could well have been the routes human beings chose to first enter the Four Corners Country.

It is not known when the first bands of hunters and gatherers discovered the mountains, mesas, and canyons of the Four Corners Country. Archaeologists believe it was later than their arrival on the Great Plains to the east or in the Great Basin to the west. The herds of large mammals, now extinct, upon which the earliest North Americans preyed may have shunned this harsh and rugged region. Probably not until the numbers of these Pleistocene mammals had dwindled did people come here to hunt the more solitary and elusive elk, sheep, and deer.

The Seasonal Round

It is thought to have been less than ten thousand years ago that the track of the first "seasonal round," the term used by anthropologists to describe the cyclical movements of hunters and gatherers throughout the world, was pressed into the Four Corners earth. For several thousand years thereafter the human imprint here was barely noticeable. Then, sometime more than two thousand years ago, the first seeds of a radically different lifeway were planted, literally and figuratively, in the Four Corners soil. The human mark deepened.

The first hunters and gatherers followed the track of the deer up from the mesas and lowlands in spring until the zenith of summer brought them to the peak of the known world. With the first touch of autumnal gold upon the tundra, the people turned and followed the path of ripening berries, swelling roots, bursting pods, and golden grasses back down the rivers toward the lowland caves and temporary camps that were their winter homes.

Life, seasons, and time followed a cyclical route, turned back upon themselves. The personally witnessed past stretched from a grandparent's first memories to a grandchild's last words.

The seasonal round was not unique to the Four Corners Country. For all but the most recent tick of the human clock, for most of two million years, all people were hunters and gatherers pursuing the seasonal round. It was, according to some anthropologists, the most successful adaptation to the environment ever known by humanity and may have been abandoned reluctantly and under great stress. Most hunters and gatherers were aware of the alternative of agriculture long before they surrendered their mobility to settle down by fixed plots of corn.

Hunting and gathering was timeless and proven, its veracity stamped by two million years of tradition upon the very genes, psyches, and souls of those people who made the first faint mark upon the Four Corners Country.

Since there were only a few small bands here, the domain of each was vast. Their technology was simple and portable but perfected by the ingenuity and testing of thousands of generations of like people who had gone before.

Mobility was the key to their success. The people carried what they owned: stone weapons of deadly sharpness, lightweight snares, nets, and atlatls, baskets of willows and grasses, clothing of the lightest furs and human-hair fabrics.

The bands moved with the flow of nature. To stand still, as the later farmers were to do, meant to resist the flow. The hunters and gatherers, if drought or early frost diminished the harvest here, moved there. If the elk and deer moved beyond the ridges, the people followed.

People moving with the cycle of the seasons are people who are not apart from nature. They would not have invented gods to bring sustenance to them, but would have moved toward regions of greater abundance based on their own knowledge of the land. Trees, streams, pebbles, people; all were equally a part of nature, equally possessed of spirit.

In the gentle green of springtime, when the canyon bottoms sang with the sound of melting snows, the people ascended to the sage rims and walked upon the mesas to the sad song of the mourning dove. Beyond the juniper forests, beckoning, were the mountain forests and the chill peaks. The bands walked slowly with their timeless chants, upward with summer.

When the sun again lit the southern ramparts of the peaks the people turned their backs on the mountains and moved down the rivers in that last clarity of summer. The first thin, grey clouds of winter hid the peaks and dimmed the sun. The deer led the way, they knew best where winter would be easiest, and the people followed. Behind them the last yellow leaves fell from the cottonwoods. Life slowed, the season further dimmed, and the first wet flakes of snow fell on the broken rims high above the people.

Spirit. All was spirit. The circle was complete.

Why, then, did the hunting and gathering bands of the Four Corners abandon their seasonal round and timeless lifeway? Theories abound. It is generally agreed that for the first several thousand years of human occupation in the region the climate was favorable to an abundance of plants and animals. These conditions fostered a greater population of hunters and gatherers than would have been possible under more arid conditions. About five thousand years ago meteorological conditions began shifting and the drier climate now characterizing the Four Corners Country began to evolve.

The slow climatic change eventually may have resulted in the first tentative attempts to cultivate plants. The population increase was another reason to explore additional means of subsistence. The people's increased aptitude at hunting may have reduced game supplies while at the same time the population was increasing and the climate was becoming less favorable.

It is not known whether knowledge of horticulture, with maize or corn as the staple crop, was the result of new peoples moving here from southern regions where farming was already practiced or whether it was gained from traders coming up from the south and instructing the people about the use of seeds. Probably traders taught the already established residents of this region.

Maize is thought to have been cultivated in the Valley of Mexico as long ago as seven thousand years, and isolated samples of maize dating back as far as five thousand years have been found in caves south of the Four Corners in New Mexico.

Archaeologists working in other parts of the world have theorized that so persistent was hunting and gathering that even if farming were adopted in a time of stress and scarcity some groups would later abandon it and return to the seasonal round as soon as conditions permitted.

In the Four Corners Country, however, agriculture was to take root permanently. The shift from hunting and gathering to the sedentary farming life was very gradual. Probably a thousand years passed from the time the first known permanent structures were built near what is now Durango, Colorado, until the subsistence pattern had shifted from primary dependence upon the seasonal round to agriculture.

Though the thousand-year shift from the mobile lifeway to fixed farm communities may have been gradual in one sense, when measured against the span of a two-million-year tradition the break was swift and radical. At first it was probably only the very young and the very old who stayed behind to tend crops; the strong and fleet continued to follow the cyclical path of the seasons.

The first known permanent homes were snug pithouses dug into the natural terraces and fertile red earth above El Río de las Animas Perdidas, the River of Lost Souls, just north of Durango. Those energy-efficient pithouses were to be the prototype for Anasazi homes throughout the Four Corners for nearly a thousand ensuing years.

As farming grew in importance, whole villages of subterranean pithouses sprang up in the middle valleys of the San Juan drainage. The valleys, broad and fertile in the elevations between 5,000 and 7,500 feet, offered the best growing conditions in the years when agriculture was taking root. Here the people, who had circled so long with the flow of the seasons, began to gather. Adequate precipitation and a long growing season must be combined for agriculture to succeed. The seasons were too short in the high country above 7,500 feet and rainfall too scarce in the basins below 5,000 feet.

Permanent settlements of pithouses and farms leapfrogged the ridges between the Animas River Valley to other tributaries of the San Juan River within the short span of a century or two. Technological changes accompanied the onset of agriculture. In addition to pithouses, there came plowing and digging sticks, hoes and other implements of change directly attributable to farming.

The old crafts, however, would not be forgotten for a long time. The baskets, so finely woven by the hunters and gatherers, continued to be perfected by the pithouse dwellers. It was the association of remnants of the magnificent baskets with the pithouses that moved nineteenth-century amateur archaeologist Richard Wetherill to name the early Anasazi peoples "Basketmakers," a name that has persisted. The later Anasazi period, following the move from the pithouses to structures built above the surface, is now referred to as the "Pueblo" phase.

Prior to their emergence from the pithouses, the Anasazi expanded their basketry skills but also began making ceramic utensils for domestic use. The switch was another reflection of the move from a technology designed to serve a mobile lifeway to one fitted to the new needs of a settled existence. Ceramics were too heavy and too fragile to carry, but they were superior to baskets for cooking and storage once permanent homes were established.

The hunters and gatherers slowly abandoned their seasonal round, but the kernels of maize contained the embryo of a new lifeway which, considering its success within the harsh environment of the Four Corners Country, was a remarkable human achievement.

There was an intangible achievement of the Anasazi, as well, which evolved over the centuries leading from the seasonal round to the building of the great towns. It was the religion of the Pueblo peoples, and it survives today among the Hopi and in New Mexico pueblos.

Though their religion, like Puebloan culture as a whole, continues to change with the times, the ceremonialism still contains dynamic elements echoing the seasonal round and the seasons themselves which turned about the first villages and plots of maize. The hunters and gatherers moved with the seasons. The seasons moved past the later farmers. Pueblo religion and ceremonialism reflect the passage of both the peoples and the seasons across the ancient homeland.

By A.D. 850 the Basketmakers were cultivating beans and squash in addition to corn. Plants native to the Four Corners were also used to satisfy food, fiber, and dye needs. A new equilibrium apparently had been established between the people and the land, though it was not to last long.

The force behind the next great shift in the Anasazi lifeway may again have been changing meteorological patterns. For a thousand years the climate had remained relatively arid. Then the Four Corners experienced an era of greater rain and snowfall. The result was that farmland in the floodplains was significantly reduced by persistently higher stream flows. Just as important, however, was that moisture in the deep, fertile soils atop the mesas increased sufficiently to allow cultivation of the tablelands high above the rivers. The greater moisture also allowed the Anasazi to move down-country into lowland basins once too arid for farming.

Within a century the Animas Valley near Durango, the apparent birthplace of Anasazi culture, was abandoned and a population explosion began on the Montelores Plateau north of Mesa Verde and in the Chaco River drainage in northwestern New Mexico.

Abandonment of the Animas Valley signaled the move by most Anasazi from pithouses to surface pueblos—stone villages—from which the Pueblo phase of the Anasazi civilization takes its name. The final architectural innovation practiced in a few scattered locations was the construction of dwellings tucked into great caves and overhangs rimming the canyons. Most of the cliff dwellings were built shortly before the Anasazi made their final lingering exodus from the San Juan River basin.

The Anasazi civilization in the San Juan was a dynamic one across space and time. Not only did the culture exhibit different characteristics with the passage of time, but also differences are obvious from place to place across the Four Corners Country. Even so, traits common to all

Anasazi at any given time allow archaeologists to consider them to have been participants in a single culture.

Archaeologists have divided the Anasazi into three major branches: The Chaco group occupied what is now the northwestern corner of New Mexico south of the San Juan River and east of the Chuska Mountains, the range that separates New Mexico from Arizona. The Kayenta branch occupied the region south of the San Juan River and west of the Chuskas in what is now northeastern Arizona. The Mesa Verde branch occupied the region north of the San Juan River in what is now southwestern Colorado and southeastern Utah.

Farming cultures did exist to the south, east, and west of the Four Corners and hunting and gathering cultures roamed beyond the perimeters of the region as well, but they are considered to have been distinct enough from the Anasazi to be cultural entities in their own right.

The Chacoan branch of the Anasazi is characterized by the magnificent architectural legacy they left behind in Chaco Culture National Historical Park. The Kayenta Anasazi are known for the ruins and ceramics left along drainages near Kayenta, Arizona. The Mesa Verdean branch is identified by the similarity of its physical legacy to the dwellings and ceramics found within Mesa Verde National Park.

As archaeological research within the Four Corners Country progresses, it is becoming apparent that the groups merged along common boundaries and that within each subregion there was a great deal of diversity as well.

It was their great diversity within a dynamic culture that explains the ability of the Anasazi to evolve and flourish for fifteen hundred years in the San Juan basin. Innovations developed and tested in one farm village soon spread to others if they could profitably be applied.

If progress can be equated with grandeur, it would have to be the Anasazi of Chaco who represented the peak of Anasazi culture. The massive, beautiful architecture of the great towns of Chaco shows some similarities to Precolumbian structures in Mexico, giving rise to a theory that cultural ties existed between the Chacoans and Meso-American cultures far to the south. Other evidence of such links includes copper bells and macaw skeletons found at Chaco which could have come only from regions encompassed by present-day Mexico.

There is evidence that not only was Chaco a major religious center for the Anasazi of northwestern New Mexico but also that a Four Corners economic system evolved around the great Chacoan towns. When people first arrived in the Chaco region, the higher elevations were forested. Today they are barren. The Chacoans consumed more than the land had to give.

One technological advance used by the Chacoans was an irrigation system that held water and delivered it to their fields. Peaceful administration of such a system would have required a parallel advance in Chacoan political and social systems, themselves radical innovations among a people so long self-reliant and decentralized.

The construction and fuel needs of the towns would have placed heavy demands on the surrounding forests. As deforestation progressed, so did soil erosion. Thus the water table would have dropped, forcing even greater reliance on rationing water. Even so, the initial success of all of the systems taken together would have allowed an increase in the Chacoan population of northwestern New Mexico.

Ultimately, local resources tapped to the limit, the Chacoans would face a choice: Leave or import resources. They chose the latter. Roads, some more than thirty miles long, lead from the deserted Chacoan towns to similar ruins in more agriculturally favorable areas to the north and south. The outlying towns indeed may have been founded to provide the center with food and fuel.

Ruins exhibiting Chacoan architectural traits have been found deep in Mesa Verdean territory in southwestern Colorado north of the San Juan River. Whether these are Chacoan trade outposts or merely evidence of Mesa Verdean fascination with Chacoan architectural fashion remains a matter of some debate among archaeologists.

By the middle of the twelfth century climate changed again. Chacoan ingenuity apparently failed to meet the challenge. The trade system may have disintegrated at this time. By the end of the century the original Chacoans were gone, thought to have migrated southward to the area now occupied by the Zunis.

The material rise of the Chacoan culture is much easier to describe than is the influence of intangibles. The simple kinship structure which had characterized hunters and gatherers had long since, among all Anasazi, evolved into more complex social, political, clan, and religious groupings.

Anasazi religion was probably directed primarily at assuring favorable weather, good crops, and harmonious relationships among people and between the people and the land. Cultural anthropologists working in other parts of the world have theorized that times of increasing environmental, economic, and social stress are characterized by a hardening of religious attitudes and more rigid ceremonialism. Similarly, peoples migrating from one region to a new land undergo a similar shift toward rigidity in their religion, sometimes adopting religious values as a means of reinforcing their own confidence during times of threat and transition. The Puritans were a later example of this phenomenon.

Possibly such a religious transformation occurred at Chaco as conditions worsened and as Meso-Americans introduced more demanding and complex cults from the south.

There is a positive factor to such a tightening of religious values; it gives the religion new definition and impetus to carry it into the future. If a religious fervor swept Chaco, then it may have helped institutionalize Anasazi religion and given it new life, explaining how it has survived among the Puebloans.

Today, as one wanders among the ruined and windswept grandeur that is Chaco, it is easy to imagine the lingering, sad departure of bands of people, trailing, singing, behind their priests, departing for a new land. There is irony to that imagery, imagined or real. Thousands of years before, the hunters and gatherers had responded to nature's flow. The Chacoans put religious, economic, and technological systems between themselves and the flow of nature. In the end, however, echoing the lifeway of their distant ancestors, they moved away from an unfavorable environment, partly of their own making, to a more benevolent region.

Time had not yet run out for the Mesa Verde and Kayenta Anasazi. Almost as if to mock the departing Chacoans, indeed perhaps linked to their departure, the Mesa Verdeans began building the magnificent cliff dwellings for which they are best known. The heartland of the Mesa Verdean culture was probably not on the Mesa Verde plateau itself but spread across the fertile crescent to the north of the plateau, stretching from the present day towns of Cortez, Colorado, to Monticello, Utah.

The crescent is the low divide between the San Juan and Dolores river valleys and it is there that the Anasazi lifeway spilled over into the Dolores Valley.

The Montelores Plateau, tilting gently toward the San Juan and cut by parallel canyons draining into the river, is ideally placed to catch the red soils blown up from the basins by spring winds. Millions of years of such winds have laid down deep and fertile topsoils atop the rocky crust of that plateau. The mesas are high enough to catch the moisture coming up from the Pacific and low enough to provide an adequate growing season for tender crops of corn, beans, and squash.

Today hundreds of thousands of acres of that plateau are planted in beans, wheat, and other dryland crops that stretch across the gentle ridges and hollows as far as the eye can see. The Anasazi farms once did the same.

The aspirations of the Mesa Verdeans appear to have been humbler than those of the Chacoans. Perhaps, because their environment was more benevolent, they never needed to develop cooperative systems on the scale reached in the Chaco Valley.

Population centers began to crystallize in the twelfth century across the rolling plateau, but there were more of them and they were smaller than those of Chaco. As the people gathered in larger centers more attention was paid to architecture and ceramic arts. This period of Mesa Verdean culture produced the enduring structures and pottery which continue to attract visitors to the Four Corners Country.

The forces of nature were shifting against the Mesa Verdeans, too. The same trend which contributed to the departure of the Chacoans was now affecting the Mesa Verdeans. By the end of the thirteenth century only a few Mesa Verdeans, scattered along the sage rims where the plateau breaks into the San Juan Valley, remained in the ancient homeland. They were the occupants of the exquisite towers seen today at Hovenweep National Monument. Most of the Mesa Verdeans had already joined the Kayentans south across the San Juan or had moved southeastward on the first leg of the epic trek across the Continental Divide toward the Rio Grande.

The Kayentans, humblest of all the Anasazi, clung to their farms in the southern San Juan Basin somewhat longer. The Kayentans developed colorful and elegant ceramics but scorned the architectural pretensions of Mesa Verde and Chaco. They kept their villages small and simple, at times clinging to the ancient pithouses as homes. Soon, however, even the undemanding Kayentans yielded to drought and arroyo cutting and abandoned the San Juan country, migrating south into what is now the domain of the Hopi.

For thousands of years the Four Corners heartland, the San Juan River basin, had been home to the Anasazi and their hunter and gatherer predecessors. Anasazi towns had spread over the middle elevations, and the human imprint deepened upon the land. Suddenly the country stood empty. Grasses and sage grew across the deserted fields, junipers took root in the sand-blown towns. Wildness reclaimed the Anasazi domain.

Just when the present era of human occupation of the Four Corners Country began is not precisely known. Utes, Navajos, and Apaches streamed into the region not long after the departure of the Anasazi. These mobile, lightfooted newcomers left little from their initial centuries here for archaeologists to ponder.

Some archaeological dating places the time of a few Navajo encampments to the fifteenth century, but that is open to debate. Navajo camps have been dated definitely to the sixteenth century.

The arrival of the first Utes in the northern San Juan country is clouded in even more mystery. Ute oral history contains accounts of interaction with the Anasazi. The first confirmed historical accounts are Hispanic records of encounters with the Utes in the late sixteenth and early seventeenth centuries. It is probable that they were here well before that.

The new arrivals initially lived more like the original hunters and gatherers than like the Anasazi. They pursued the seasonal round, lived in temporary shelters, and moved as climatic conditions demanded. Where the recently departed Anasazi had beseeched the gods to look favorably upon their fields, the newcomers asked only that their feet carry them to the best hunting and harvesting grounds.

For the Navajos, their arrival marked not only the end of a long journey down from the far north but the dawn of a new cultural era. Their encounters with the Anasazi Puebloans of the Rio Grande and Hopi villages, though not always peaceful, introduced them to the radical concepts of agriculture and permanent homes. Soon, showing the same genius for synthesis and assimilation for which they are known today, the Navajos were experimenting with farms and homes of their own.

The Navajo hogan, still in use today, evolved and fields were planted in the canyon bottoms south of the San Juan River. Navajos gradually combined farming with the nomadic traditions, which they have pursued into the twentieth century. Nevertheless, a unique adaptation of Anasazi ways had found its way back into the Four Corners where it had ruled for so long.

The sparse and mobile bands of Utes claimed the rugged San Juan highlands north of the river as their domain. The Jicarilla Apaches, linguistic cousins to the Navajo, made their stronghold the headlands of the Navajo River which flows into the upper San Juan from the east. Where it all would have led—this new relationship between Ute, Navajo, Apache, and Puebloan—can now be only a matter of speculation.

The Conquerors

Far east of the dawn the rulers of Spain agreed to finance a search for a new route to the Orient. The result was that Columbus stumbled upon the "New World" instead in 1492. The grandchildren of Puebloan, Ute, Navajo, and Apache infants living in the Four Corners Country at that fateful instant were destined to feel the shock waves of a cultural firestorm that was to break against the stony ramparts of the Four Corners Country before exhausting itself.

In 1520 Cortez conquered the Aztecs and the Valley of Mexico. The Spaniards then turned the forces of conquest north and south. In 1540 Coronado gave the Puebloans their first traumatic introduction to Spanish culture then moving inexorably northward from Mexico City.

By the end of the sixteenth century Oñate had established the first Spanish settlement in the Province of New Mexico at the confluence of the Chama River with the Rio Grande at what is now called San Juan Pueblo. It would be another quarter century before the Pilgrims landed at Plymouth Rock. The Four Corners was claimed for Spain, and the Chama River would provide a route into the center of the region.

Oñate's settlement at the mouth of the Chama River was the capital of New Mexico Province until 1610 when the provincial headquarters were moved to the newly founded town of Santa Fe.

It is safe to assume that the Apaches, Utes, and Navajos would have found the concept of themselves as Spanish subjects bewildering at best. In reality, though the Four Corners was within the Spanish borders, it would be centuries before permanent European settlements would be established. The territorially alert Native Americans kept the newcomers out. Four Corners Country was destined to become one of the last frontiers in North America.

The opening decades of Spanish rule of the Puebloan descendants of the Anasazi were brutal. The Hopis, after an initial flirtation, cast the Spanish out and successfully resisted their return. The Rio Grande pueblos absorbed the early Spanish determination to wipe out the timeless Anasazi/Pueblo religion and culture and replace them with Christianity and European political structures. Pueblo Indian religion responded by literally going underground. Ceremonies continued in the kivas, or ceremonial chambers, found in each pueblo.

The long-term result of early Spanish threats to the Puebloan lifeway may have been, as with the stresses and uncertainty that accompanied the Anasazi exodus from the San Juan River Basin, to strengthen the culture in the face of threats from the Spanish and, later, from the dominant American culture.

The Spaniards arrived in New Mexico Province with material possessions and technology that should have given them great advantage over their Native American "subjects": horses, firearms, the wheel, metal tools, sheep, and cattle. Despite these attributes of European culture, the Spanish hold on the province remained precarious. The Spanish soldiers and colonists were few in number, and they were far removed from the capitals of Madrid and Mexico City.

The Puebloans lacked some of the strengths of European culture but they possessed one advantage of far greater power: Theirs was a lifeway merged over thousands of years with the place itself. The Spanish were aliens in an unforgiving land. In the end the Spanish colonists in New Mexico would adapt elements of the Puebloan lifeway to their own as a means to their survival. The Native Americans, on the other hand, would pick and choose among elements of European culture and adopt only those of greatest benefit to them. Their most valuable acquisition from the Spanish, who gave it reluctantly, was the horse.

Spanish bureaucrats in Mexico City and Madrid were fearful that their colonists in New Mexico would assume so many Native American ways that they would become more Puebloan than Spaniard. That would only weaken colonial loyalty to the crown. The same bureaucrats knew, too, that the pioneers were virtually defenseless should the Native Americans decide to drive them from their remote outposts. These two fears led Madrid to issue edicts forbidding Spanish exploration and trade expeditions into the Ute and Navajo domains in the Four Corners.

Despite the official bans, the Spanish frontiersmen, as frontiersmen do anywhere, pursued the necessary course to assure survival. They entered the Ute domain in pursuit of trade.

For decades the sedentary Puebloans of the Rio Grande Valley appeared to accept the Spanish presence, oppressive though it was. The fierce Apaches and Navajos simply took what they wanted from the vulnerable colonists and became more powerfully hostile in the process. The Utes seemed to scorn all trappings of European culture except horses and firearms.

The horse enabled the nomadic Native Americans to expand vastly the scope of their domains. Soon cultures that always had been separated by rugged terrain collided, and an era of unprecedented conflict dawned. The Native American nations, with the exception of the Utes who played a swing role in the balance of power, fought with one another and against the Spaniards.

One apparent reason for the docility of the Rio Grande Puebloans in the face of the Spanish conquest was their timeless tradition of town autonomy. The pueblos seemed unable to unite, a necessity if the Spanish were to be driven from the Four Corners Country.

But in 1680, Pueblo towns from Taos to Hopi Oraibi came together and drove the Spanish from the Province of New Mexico. The alien flag that had flown for more than eighty years was lowered as the Spanish fled.

Pueblo tradition soon overcame unity and their brief alliance weakened. In 1692, led by Diego de Vargas, the Spanish returned to Santa Fe, the Reconquest achieved. One reason for Puebloan acceptance of the return of the Spanish may have been the increasingly effective raids on their villages by Comanche and Navajo horsemen. The Puebloans needed the Spanish presence to help fend off the invaders. The Spanish, in turn, needed Puebloan assistance if they themselves were to hold off the Navajos and Comanches.

De Vargas, sensing the precariousness of the Reconquest, introduced somewhat more enlightened policies toward Pueblo religious and social life. Thus, in the end, the 1680 Revolt may have achieved its goal—the survival of a religion and lifeway deeply rooted in the land.

With the dawn of the eighteenth century, Spanish farm villages were pushing up the tributaries of the Rio Grande, including the Chama River. The Chama was destined to become the route followed by Hispanic traders into the Utes' San Juan domain, even though the official ban on entering that forbidden territory remained rigidly in effect even after the Reconquest.

The physical appearance of the eighteenth-century Hispanic villages differed so little from the ancient adobe Pueblo towns that a stranger wandering through the countryside may have had trouble telling them apart. A new frontier culture was emerging from the blending of Spanish and Pueblo civilizations, a culture uniquely New Mexican.

The Chama River rises among the towering peaks of the San Juan Mountains east of the Continental Divide. Just west of the Divide the Navajo River begins its course toward the San Juan. One point on the Divide between the two rivers dips to form a low saddle.

Spaniards wishing to cross the Divide seem inevitably to have been drawn to that saddle. It was along this route—up the Chama and down the Navajo rivers—a route probably used by the Anasazi in earlier times, that the illicit New Mexican traders entered Ute territory.

On a bluff overlooking the Chama River is the eighteenth-century Spanish village of Abiquiu. A region of indescribable beauty, it is a place haunted by the intrigue marking its past. Abiquiu prospered as the irreverent outfitter of illegal expeditions headed into the San Juan country. It was inevitable that New Mexican traders returning from those forays should bring with them reports of the mineral-rich mountains and fertile mesas and valleys lying beyond the Divide.

But Spanish authorities and Utes alike did not weaken in their resistance to a permanent Hispanic presence beyond the Divide. The Utes were as strong as ever in their regard of the earth as sacred. To allow the mountains and mesas to be gouged by pick and plow would have been the worst form of blasphemy.

Inevitably, however, rumors of wealth reached eager ears in Mexico and Spain. In 1761 Spanish authorities gave in and allowed the first official exploration of the San Juan country. The exploration was led by Juan de Rivera. By 1765 he had made three trips into the region.

Rivera's sketchy journal accounts of his expeditions were recently discovered in a Madrid archive. An analysis of the records by historian Donald Cutter provides evidence that Rivera was far from the first to enter the San Juan country. Cutter concluded that many Spanish names for major landforms within the San Juan country had been in place long before Rivera's arrival on the scene. Hispanic names for the mountains, rivers, and buttes north of the San Juan River are a timeless reminder of the New Mexican pioneers who befriended the Utes centuries ago.

Rivera had officially opened what was to become known as the Spanish Trail. While Rivera was marveling at the sights beyond the Divide, Spanish religious and military authorities were establishing a chain of missions along the California coast from Monterey to San Francisco. A link between the 150-year-old capital of Santa Fe and the new missions was imperative.

Hostile Navajos and Hopis stood in the way of a southern route to the Pacific Coast. The only hope of a direct link was to travel through Ute territory and then to push on through the terra incognita beyond to San Francisco Bay.

In July 1776 two priests, Francisco V. Domínguez and Silvestre Vélez de Escalante, led a party of explorers past the palace in Santa Fe north toward Abiquiu on the first leg of a journey to map that route to the Pacific. The fathers must have glanced with pride at the flag of Spain as they rode away at the head of their party in anticipation of what lay ahead.

The proud party could not have known that in Philadelphia, two thousand miles to the east, the British colonies had declared their independence from the English throne, signaling the end to colonialism in the New World. Domínguez and Escalante could not have known, either, what ordeals and failures awaited them on the rugged trail.

Escalante's journal of the expedition has become a southwestern classic. After the party crossed the Divide it headed along the old Spanish Trail down the Navajo to the San Juan River. They veered northward along the trail, passed the edge of present-day Durango, and explored Anasazi towns to the west.

Upon reaching the foot of the Mesa Verde and viewing the vast, canyon-gashed sage plain beyond, Escalante's recorded enthusiasms began to wane. As autumn turned to winter the explorers had forged westward only to central Utah, less than halfway to San Francisco. Weakened by injuries and illness and faced with mutiny, the two priests turned back, crossed the Colorado River at the Crossing of the Fathers, and arrived in Santa Fe at Christmas. Later, agents of Spain picked up where Domínguez and Escalante gave up and succeeded in forging a link between Santa Fe and Monterey.

In 1821, three hundred years after Cortez overthrew Montezuma, the Mexican Revolution ended Spanish rule of Mexico and New Mexico Province. The Four Corners Country became the northern frontier of the Republic of Mexico. In reality, little changed. The Utes, Navajos, and Hopis defended their domains with more vigilance than ever.

In 1848 the United States wrested control of New Mexico from Mexico and the Stars and Stripes were raised over the palace in Santa Fe. The Utes and Navajos regarded this change as they had earlier conquests. In the Four Corners Country little changed.

By 1869, however, new winds were blowing across the rocky ramparts separating the Four Corners Country from the United States as a whole. The Utes were being pushed south by settlers in northern Colorado. The San Juan country became their impenetrable stronghold, off limits even to transient wanderers who were not Ute.

A few prospectors entered the San Juan highlands and returned with exaggerated tales of mineral wealth. A boom seemed imminent, its target the upper reaches of the Animas River where Silverton is now located. The Utes, the terrain, and the outbreak of the Civil War combined to discourage any attempt at mining.

In 1863, Kit Carson arrived south of the San Juan River with a large detachment of troops, burning Navajo fields and killing their stock as part of a campaign to drive the Navajos from their centuries-old homeland. The culmination of his cruel assault was the forced Long Walk out of the Four Corners. Many Navajos died along the way. In 1868, admitting the failure of their Navajo policy, the government allowed the people to return to their homes.

The Utes were to fare as badly. In 1870 Coloradans east of the Divide were glancing enviously at the minerals and fertile lands on the rugged Ute reservation. In 1873 four million acres along the Animas River north of Durango were sliced from the Ute domain. The opening of the San Juan country set off a rush of prospectors over the Divide. The town of Silverton was founded in 1874 in a mountain park surrounded by towering peaks alongside the Animas River. For the first time since the departure of the Anasazi, permanent settlements began springing up in the heart of the Four Corners Country.

The modern era swept across the region like a storm.

Seekers of Wealth

Within less than a decade the Utes had been pushed into a thin, arid strip of reservation south of the mountains that they had roamed for so long. The Jicarilla Apaches were confined to a reservation along the Navajo River, a domain far too small to support their mobile lifeway. The Navajos were allowed to keep some of their domain south of the San Juan, and the Rio Grande Puebloans were given small reservations around their ancient communities.

A major achievement of the Native Americans of the Four Corners Country had been to hold the modern era at bay until most other regions of the American West were "tamed." The Four Corners Country was a last frontier.

With the opening of the San Juan region, the New Mexicans of the Chama Valley settled along the old Spanish Trail to what is now Durango. Their arrival was quiet and their lives deeply traditional. Their San Juan farms and villages resembled the old pueblos of the Rio Grande. It was as if the Anasazi had come home. The New Mexicans joined the Native Americans as a traditional Four Corners culture attempting to preserve proven ways of living while trying to soften the impact of a new and conquering culture upon an ancient land and its people. The rights and dignity of the New Mexicans were subjected to the same cruel betrayal by the arriving U.S. settlers as had been those of the Native Americans.

While the Native Americans were holding back the newcomers, the United States as a whole was in the throes of a revolutionary shift from its own agrarian culture to an increasingly centralized and urbanized culture.

By the final quarter of the nineteenth century mass production, specialization, railroads, and the telegraph had already transformed American culture into a highly centralized one. The automobile, telephone, and electric power were just around the corner. Capital rather than individual entrepreneurship would be the determining force of the future.

It was then that the Four Corners Country was opened to modern development, after its destiny was firmly in the hands of corporations and urban financing groups far from the raw materials upon which their fortunes rested.

The schism between ownership and labor, too, had become a reality before the opening of the Four Corners Country. Thus the taming of the Four Corners frontier was a corporate affair. The names of very few pioneers stand out as having influenced the shape of the region.

Modern agriculture arrived in the Four Corners Country later than in other regions of the West. The days of the cattle baron were already over. The Homestead Act was in effect. Mechanization had taken the place of human labor on farms, and transportation advances were making the economies of scale as important in agriculture as in other segments of the economy, even in the Four Corners.

Tourism was already an important industry by the time the narrow gauge steam railroads had crossed the Divide into the San Juan region. The frontier had been romanticized and marketed by American and European writers. The rugged Four Corners Country attracted the writers, artists, and photographers needed to keep the frontier myth alive. They found everything they could ask: sheer mountains, shadowy canyons, Indians, mining camps, narrow gauge railroads, and those mysterious Anasazi towns.

Thus modern culture did not evolve within the Four Corners Country as it had across the rest of the nation. It arrived overnight in post-adolescent form.

The mineral-laden fluids that had bubbled up and cooled into metal-flecked veins of quartz in the San Juan dome tens of millions of years before drew people into the Four Corners Country like a magnet. Countless prospectors, promoters, and laborers poured into the high San Juans. The towns of Ouray, Rico, Telluride, Creede, Lake City, and Durango soon joined Silverton as mining centers. Their ornate Victorian architecture still holds great appeal.

Only a handful of the hopeful horde ever struck it rich. The rest left the San Juans for the Sierras or the Yukon in search of the elusive mother lode. Some wandered down the valleys and homesteaded atop forgotten Anasazi farms where the seasons, the soil, and rainfall favored their crops.

A few Latter Day Saints lowered their wagons through the Hole in the Rock on the Colorado River and pushed up the San Juan River to colonize Bluff and the rugged canyon bottoms of southeastern Utah. Soon even those remote desert strongholds were greening beneath the waters brought from the rivers by the ingenious Mormons.

In 1880 the Denver & Rio Grande Railway extended its narrow gauge tracks westward into the San Juan region. In 1881 the tracks joined the old Spanish Trail over the Divide and followed it on to Durango. The railroad reached its ultimate goal, Silverton, in 1882. Tourists now take the scenic ride from Durango to Silverton.

Cattle ranches spread upriver from the deserted Anasazi ruins near Dolores. Timber harvesters felled the towering stands of ponderosa pine that stretched unbroken across the foothills where the mesas meet the mountains. Orchards spread along the middle valley of the San Juan and up its tributaries. Water from the Dolores River was diverted to irrigate a part of the vast plateau stretching northward from Mesa Verde. More rail lines pushed west and south from Durango to serve the farm, ranch, timber, and mining towns. Sheep grazed the mountain tundra, and plows turned the sage where the Anasazi once had farmed. But it was gold, silver, and copper that had launched the modern era in the Four Corners and it was mineral wealth that continued to dominate the economy into the twentieth century.

If it was absentee ownership that financed the booms, it was immigrants who did the work. Laborers from the Slavic kingdoms, Sweden, Austria, Italy, Ireland, Cornwall, Wales, and China poured off the oncoming trains and into the boarding houses, mines, and mills. When they could afford to, they sent for their families. The immigrants were the ones, when the booms went bust, who stayed to keep the towns alive. They left a rich cultural, cosmopolitan stamp on the high-country towns which is evident today.

If capital could be poured into the San Juans it could just as easily be withdrawn, and it was. Mines closed, payrolls withered. The ebb and flow of prosperity and poverty across the high country touched the Four Corners as a whole and set an economic pattern which persists.

The booms and busts continue to roll over the Four Corners with a new twist; they are no longer centered only in the mountains but move back and forth from the coal-rich basins, to the uranium-stained canyons, to the oil beneath the mesas, to the metallic mountains, and back again. Well into the twentieth century modern culture has remained unrooted and alien, not subject to the circle of the seasons, sky, and earth but subject, instead, to the seasons of distant profits, wars, and economic cycles.

If there was any stability to human life in the Four Corners Country it was found within the traditional cultures—among the Utes, Navajos, Apaches, Pueblos, and New Mexicans—who subsisted on little and asked as little of the land as it had to give.

Epilogue

The traumatic arrival of the modern era brought with it an unprecedented level of conflict between ancient and new cultures and between the newcomers and the land.

Newcomers were filled with a cultural arrogance born of their technological strength. The Native Americans were conquered and held captive on reservations. The New Mexicans were the subject of virulent bigotry and political betrayal. Vigilantes drove them from their farms and ranches, deprived them of their civil rights, and hounded them into poverty.

Unlike the ancient cultures, the modern culture was not self-sufficient but inextricably tied to the national and world economy. So, even as the newcomers were taking the most productive areas of the Four Corners Country for themselves, their destinies really were controlled by abstract systems whose centers lay far beyond the mountains. The abandoned Chacoan economic network paled to nothingness in comparison.

The traditional cultures began succumbing to the new way. The Navajos increased the size of their flocks and drove their sheep into the most remote corners of the canyon country where the grass was consumed to its roots. Within a few decades the land was bare beneath the spring winds and autumn cloudbursts, and hardships as great as those visited by Kit Carson again descended upon the people.

The Ute bands resisted agriculture a while longer before some agreed to plow the earth. The Weminuche band of Utes was so angered by this that they left the banks of the Pine River near Ignacio and moved west beyond Mesa Verde, in the shadow of Ute Mountain, to Towaoc where they live today.

Mines, mills, smelters, and sawmills spewed their wastes into the rivers and sky. Lumbermen chewed their way through the vast, towering forests on the foothills, then turned their saws against the steep stands of spruce and fir rising toward timberline.

Sheep and cattle overgrazed the high country tundra in the summer and the fragile canyon bottoms in winter. Plows broke the grassy mesa tops beneath the harsh spring winds.

The crystal clear rivers ran grey from mine wastes and then red from the bleeding earth washed from the plowed mesas and clearcut slopes. Before long the easiest resources were gone. What is left is harder and costlier to wrench from the earth. Capital migrated elsewhere.

The children of the newcomers followed the money back over the mountains, lured by the bright lights and promise of the cities. A silence fell over the wounded land. The boom had gone bust.

More booms were to follow. After World War II and the birth of the atomic age, prospectors poured into the rugged canyon country, gouging roads with bulldozers, in search of uranium. A brief flurry of mining and milling followed, bringing new wealth to small-town merchants and raising the hopes of farm villages.

No sooner had the boom gone inevitably bust than came the oil boom of the fifties. Editors and promoters were inspired to even greater epidemics of boom fever. As usual, many shirts were lost.

By the mid-seventies, there was no longer any attempt to differentiate between coal, oil, gas, and uranium. Now it was the energy boom. That boom has come and gone and come and gone again.

Each boom leaves behind new roads pushed into wild country, lifeless heaps of slag and waste, rusted webs of iron, and vacant, staring storefronts along the main streets. Each boom is followed by that silence while the money and promoters move on.

By the early nineteen eighties a new tourist boom was rolling across the Four Corners Country. Most of the high-country mining towns have been transformed into second-home communities for summer residents and winter skiers. Mining claims in the mountains have become cabin sites, and the verdant mesas and valleys have been cut up into countless lots where town dwellers can raise a horse.

One of the great ironies of the tourist boom is its role in rewriting the history of the Four Corners Country. The gunslingers and posses that inhabit pulp westerns and Hollywood backlots were never a part of the history of this region. Yet, taking their cue from Gunsmoke and Bonanza, the summer entrepreneurs who line the streets of the more picturesque towns with plywood falsefronts and wooden Indians are hawking a past that never was. In an age when tourists are interested in historical accuracy it is this shallow greediness that will prove to be the rubber hatchet that kills the golden goose.

The booms do go bust; they do leave scars on the magnificent face of this place. The boom and bust pattern—accompanied by rootless and alienated people seeking quick profits—will persist.

But even the booms have endowed the Four Corners Country with a slowly accumulating legacy whose richness is just becoming apparent. For each ten newcomers departing in the wake of a boom, one stays.

The few who stay are here not because of dreams of wealth but because of a deep love of the land into which they wandered. Slowly they and their descendants are growing in numbers and are becoming a force marshalled against the excesses of their own heritage.

They have turned their backs on the booms and have found ways to subsist here as well as possible in today's systemized world. They are held here by the land and are now defenders of this region's cruel but beautiful wilderness.

Here today are the children of the Native Americans, the New Mexicans, and the immigrants. They regard the land as something more than a source of enough money to get the hell out and go back to the city. They have learned the lessons of the booms and no longer trust them. They believe that to avoid the busts one does not ask more of the land than it has to give. Every year they are joined by a few more newcomers drawn here by the beauty and their own willingness to sacrifice.

It is this new culture, legacy of past booms and ancient cultures, which is at last finding its own voice. These are the people who fight against opening more wilderness to development and killing more rivers. They sit for long, tiring hours in stuffy hearing rooms arguing for better lumbering techniques, for less mining and power plant pollution, for better land reclamation practices in the wake of the stripminers. They have a long fight ahead of them.

But already the rivers are running clearer, the pine forests are coming back, the skies are bluer. Farmers are turning to soil conservation. Game herds are growing. The scars are healing. Tens of millions of acres of wilderness remain roadless and untouched across the mountains, mesas, and canyons of the Four Corners Country.

Those who call the Four Corners Country home face the prospect of continuing struggle. The conflict is less the old one of culture against culture and technology against the land. Now the conflict is within ourselves and against our age-old inclination to ask more of this place than it has to give. This struggle is now shared by most who are here. New alliances are forming, old prejudices are disappearing.

There will never be many of us here. The forces which shape the land give little to human communities. Not many can stay and survive. We are learning not to fight what we can't change. We are beginning to flow with the circle of the seasons, to walk those ancient pathways linking mountain to mesa to canyon—if not with our feet, then at least with our spirits.

Acknowledgments

Without the cooperation and assistance of professionals with the National Park Service, the Center for Southwest Studies at Fort Lewis College in Durango, Colorado, and the Crow Canyon Archaeological Center in Cortez, Colorado, completion of this book would not have been possible. The author deeply appreciates the solitude and encouragement provided by Ed and Jo Berger of Cortez, Colorado.

The publication of this book was assisted by a grant from the Edna Rider Whiteman Foundation.

Bibliography

Ambler, J. Richard. *The Anasazi: Prehistoric People of the Four Corners Region*, photography by Marc Gaede, Museum of Northern Arizona, Flagstaff, 1977.

Aveni, Anthony F., editor. *Archeoastronomy in Precolumbian America*, University of Texas Press, 1975.

Baars, Donald L. *Geology of the Canyons of the San Juan River*, Four Corners Geological Society, 1973.

————. *Red Rock Country*, Doubleday/Natural History Press, 1972.

Berger, Joanne H. and Edward F., editors. *Insights Into the Ancient Ones*, Crow Canyon Center, Cortez, Colorado, 1980.

Bolton, Herbert. *A Pageant in the Wilderness*, Utah State Historical Society, 1950.

Bradish, B. B. "Geology of the Monument Upwarp," Four Corners Geological Society Symposium, 1952.

Colorado Water Conservation Board and U.S. Department of Agriculture. *Water and Related Land Resources of the San Juan River Basin of Arizona, Colorado, New Mexico, and Utah*, U.S. Forest Service, 1974.

Cutter, Donald C. "Prelude to a Pageant in the Wilderness," Western Historical Quarterly, Vol. 8, January, 1977.

Delaney, Robert W. *The Southern Ute People*, Indian Tribal Series, Phoenix, 1974.

Eggan, Fred. *The American Indian, Perspectives for the Study of Social Change*, Aldine, 1966.

————. *Social Organization of the Western Pueblos*, University of Chicago Press, 1950.

Erdman, James A., C. L. Douglas, and J. W. Marr. *Environment of Mesa Verde, Colorado*, National Park Service, 1969.

Euler, Robert C., G. J. Gumerman, T.N.V. Karlstrom, J. S. Dean, and R. H. Hevly. "The Colorado Plateaus: Cultural Dynamics and Paleoenvironment," Science, Vol. 205, pp. 1089−1101, 1979.

Gaede, Marnie (editor) and Marc Gaede (photogapher). *Camera, Spade and Pen*, University of Arizona Press, 1980.

Gregory, H. E. "Geology of the Navajo Country," U.S. Geological Survey Professional Paper 93, 1917.

———— . "The San Juan Country," U.S. Geological Survey Professional Paper 188, 1938.

Hyde, Philip (text by Stephen Jett). *Navajo Wildlands*, Sierra Club, 1967.

Kessell, John L. *Kiva, Cross and Crown: The Pecos Indians and New Mexico, 1540 – 1840*, National Park Service, 1979.

Kidder, A. V. *An Introduction to the Study of Southwestern Archeology*, Yale University Press, 1962.

Lange, Charles H. *Cochiti: A New Mexico Pueblo Past and Present*, University of Texas Press, 1959.

Lévi-Strauss, Claude. *The Raw and the Cooked*, Harper & Row, 1969.

Lohman, S. W. *The Geologic Story of Canyonlands National Park*, Geological Survey Bulletin 1327, 1974.

Longacre, William A., editor. *Reconstructing Prehistoric Pueblo Societies*, A School of American Research Book, University of New Mexico Press, 1970.

McConnell, Virginia. "Captain Baker and the San Juan Humbug," Colorado Magazine, The Colorado Historical Society, Vol. 48, Winter 1971.

Martin, Paul S. and Fred Plog. *The Archeology of Arizona*, Doubleday/Natural History Press, 1973.

O'Rourke, Paul M. *Frontiers in Transition: A History of Southwestern Colorado*, Bureau of Land Management, 1980.

Ortiz, Alphonso. *The Tewa World*, University of Chicago Press, 1969.

Osborne, Douglas. "Slow Exodus from Mesa Verde," Natural History, Vol. 85, pp. 38 – 45, 1976.

Parsons, Elsie Clews. *Pueblo Indian Religion*, University of Chicago Press, 2 vols., 1939.

Pike, Donald G. *Anasazi: Ancient People of the Rock*, American West, 1974.

Reyman, Jonathan. "Astronomy, Architecture, and Adaptation at Pueblo Bonito," Science, Vol. 193, pp. 957 – 62, 1976.

———— . "Mexican Influence on Southwest Ceremonialism," Ph.D. Thesis, 1971, Southern Illinois University.

Rippeteau, Bruce Estes. *A Colorado Book of the Dead, the Prehistoric Era*, Colorado Historical Society, 1979.

Rohn, Arthur H. *Mug House*, National Park Service, 1971 (second printing, INTERpark, Cortez, Colorado, 1983).

Smith, Duane. *Rocky Mountain Boomtown: A History of Durango*, University of New Mexico Press, 1980.

Spicer, Edward H. *Perspectives in American Indian Culture Change*, University of Chicago Press, 1961.

Stephen, Alexander M. *Hopi Journal*, edited by Elsie Clews Parsons, Columbia University Contributions to Anthropology, 1936.

Swadesh, Frances Leon. *Los Primeros Pobladores*, Notre Dame, 1974.

Thompson, Ian M. "The Silverton Country: A Historical Sketch," Four Corners Geological Society, 1974.

Vivian, Gordon and Paul Reiter. "The Great Kivas of Chaco Canyon and Their Relationships," School of American Research and Museum of New Mexico Monograph 22, 1960.

I also have interviewed people with professional or occupational knowledge of the natural and cultural history of the region.

The Photographs

Storm, Monument Basin, Utah

50

Mill, Mayday, Colorado

Taos Pueblo, New Mexico

53

Black Canyon of the Gunnison, Colorado

54

Lime Creek, Colorado

Hillside near Mayday, Colorado

Monument Valley from Utah 163, Utah

Bear Creek tributary, Colorado

Footbridge, Periman's Farm, Colorado

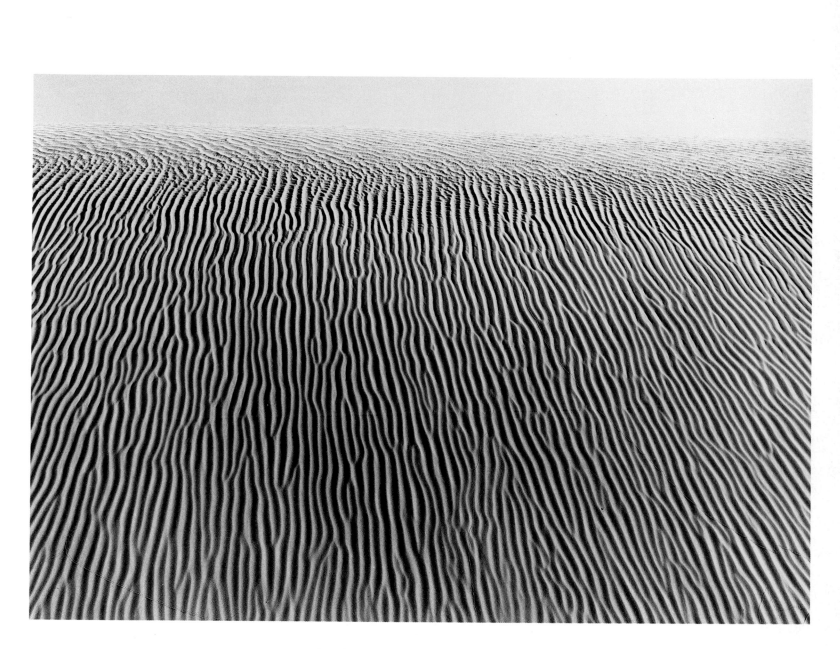

Sand dunes, Canyon de Chelly, Arizona

Hailstorm, Canyon de Chelly, Arizona

Desert varnish, Monument Valley, Arizona

64   Tower Arch, Arches National Park, Utah

Soda Springs Basin, Utah

Whale Rock, Canyonlands, Utah

The Thumb, Monument Valley, Arizona

West Needles, Colorado

Clover and Gambel oak, Dolores Canyon, Colorado

Navajo Springs, Colorado

71

The "Blade," Canyon de Chelly, Arizona

Gambel oak, Salt Creek, Canyonlands, Utah

La Sal Mountains from Little Bridge Canyon, Utah

Green River Overlook, Canyonlands, Utah

Dead juniper, Cedar Mesa, Utah

Pueblo del Arroyo, Chaco Culture Park, New Mexico

Betatakin, Navajo National Monument, Arizona

Square Tower and Hackberry, Hovenweep, Utah

Church wall, Jemez Springs, New Mexico

Pool hall, Antonito, Colorado

Wall, Los Ojos, New Mexico

Gandy dancers, Monte Vista, Colorado

Children, Los Ojos, New Mexico

Gomez Store, Pagosa Junction, Colorado

Taxidermist's, Monte Vista, Colorado

Haystacks, Echo Basin, Colorado

Ismay Trading Post, Colorado

Oil storage tank, Aneth, Colorado

Trailer, Fort Defiance, Arizona

Victorian storefront, Rico, Colorado

Silverton, Colorado, 1980

96

Church at Trampas, New Mexico

Cemetery, Monte Vista, Colorado

Pagosa Springs, Colorado

Shiprock, New Mexico

Farm, New Mexico 126

Coal elevator, Navajo Reservation, Arizona

Junction of Highways 285 and 368, Colorado

Navajo steppe country, Utah

Four Corners Monument

Condominiums, Telluride, Colorado

Horses, Navajo Reservation, Utah

Picuris Pueblo, New Mexico

Molas Divide, Colorado

Bottles, Ismay Trading Post, Colorado

White House Ruin Trail, Canyon de Chelly, Arizona